CONTENTS

Blessed Assurance

Lyrics by Fanny J. Crosby
Music by Phoebe Palmer Knapp
Arranged by Glenda Austin

Unhurried, with expression

Pedal as needed

rit.

Light Gospel Rock (with steady beat)

SOLOS FOR THE SANCTUARY
HYMNS 2
10 PIANO SOLOS FOR THE CHURCH PIANIST

Arranged by Glenda Austin

ISBN 978-1-5400-5629-0

WILLIS MUSIC

EXCLUSIVELY DISTRIBUTED BY

HAL•LEONARD®

Visit Hal Leonard Online at
www.halleonard.com

Contact us:
Hal Leonard
7777 West Bluemound Road
Milwaukee, WI 53213
Email: info@halleonard.com

In Europe, contact:
Hal Leonard Europe Limited
42 Wigmore Street
Marylebone, London, W1U 2RN
Email: info@halleonardeurope.com

In Australia, contact:
Hal Leonard Australia Pty. Ltd.
4 Lentara Court
Cheltenham, Victoria, 3192 Australia
Email: info@halleonard.com.au

PREFACE

Many of these arrangements began years ago as a young teen, playing a little spinet piano at our church, the Friendship Baptist Church—the name says it all! I am still playing, though I've moved to the Methodist Church. My sister Gloria and I have been playing piano and organ duets for more than FIFTY YEARS! That's even hard for me to comprehend.

All the hymns included in this book have been "tested" as preludes, offertories, postludes, or special solos. Please use them as you feel led. Seldom do I play anything the same way twice, so feel free to make these arrangements your own and to stylize them to your liking!

May God bless you as you use your talents to serve the Lord. "As each has received a gift, use it to serve one another, as good stewards of God's varied grace." (1 Peter 4:10)

Glenda Austin

For my mom, Audrey

Great Is Thy Faithfulness

Words by Thomas O. Chisholm
Music by William M. Runyan
Arranged by Glenda Austin

With reverence, freely

Pedal as needed

For Sharon Thigpen Callahan

Jesus Paid It All

Words by Elvina M. Hall
Music by John T. Grape
Arranged by Glenda Austin

With reverence and conviction

Holy, Holy, Holy

Text by Reginald Heber
Music by John B. Dykes
Arranged by Glenda Austin

Just As I Am

Words by Charlotte Elliott
Music by William B. Bradbury
Arranged by Glenda Austin

Nothing but the Blood

Words and Music by Robert Lowry
Arranged by Glenda Austin

Praise the Lord! Ye Heavens Adore Him!

By Rowland Prichard
Arranged by Glenda Austin

*This hymn is also known as "Come, Thou Long Expected Jesus."

To God Be the Glory

Words by Fanny J. Crosby
Music by William H. Doane
Arranged by Glenda Austin

With great declaration!

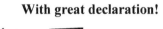

Pedal as needed

Turn Your Eyes Upon Jesus/
Softly and Tenderly

Softly and Tenderly
Words and Music by Will L. Thompson
Turn Your Eyes Upon Jesus
Words and Music by Helen H. Lemmel
Arranged by Glenda Austin

For Heather Hearn Rathnau

Trust and Obey

Words by John H. Sammis
Music by Daniel B. Towner
Arranged by Glenda Austin